PRECIOUS EARTH

Waste
and Recycling

Jen Green

Chrysalis Education

US publication copyright © 2004 Chrysalis Education
International copyright reserved in all countries.
No part of this book may be reproduced in any
form without written permission from the publisher.

Distributed in the United States by
Smart Apple Media
1980 Lookout Drive
North Mankato, Minnesota 56003

Copyright © Chrysalis Books Group Plc 2004

Library of Congress Control Number: 2003116147

ISBN 1-59389-137-7

Editorial Manager: Joyce Bentley

Produced by
Tall Tree Ltd.
Designer: Ed Simkins
Editor: Kate Simkins
Consultant: Michael Rand
Picture Researcher: Lorna Ainger

Printed in Hong Kong

Some of the more unfamiliar words used in this book
are explained in the glossary on page 31.

Photo Credits:
Alamy/Lonnie Duka: front cover br, 27t, Ken Hawkins:
front cover c, 10, 30, David Hoffman: front cover c,
back cover, 6, Steve Skjold 5t,
Robert Battersby/Tografox 8, 9, 17b, 23t, 27b
Corbis/Jeff Albertson 20, James L. Amos 1, 22, Yann
Arthus-Bertrand 16, Tom Stewart 26, Natalie Fobes
23b, Gehl Company 14, Nick Hawkes/Ecoscene 15b,
Ed Kashi 13t, Rob Lewine 7b, Richard Hamilton Smith
11t, Getty Images/Hugh Burden 18
Ed Simkins 28t, Still Pictures/Mark Edwards: front cover
tr, 2, 11b, 17t, 21t, 31, Julio Etchart: front cover tl, 5b,
Peter Frischmuth 24, Gayo 15t, Philippe Hays 13b,
19b, Robert J. Ross 25t, Kevin Schafer 19t, Hartmut
Schwarzbach 4.

Contents

What a waste!

Every hour of every day, we produce waste as we eat, drink, and go about our lives. The waste produced by everyone adds up to a huge amount. We have to get rid of this waste through a process called waste disposal.

Houses, schools, stores, and offices all make waste. So do farms and factories. If waste is not disposed of safely, it can pollute nature and harm people and wildlife. As the number of people in the world increases, so the problem of waste disposal is growing, too. Waste can be a solid, such as garbage, a liquid, such as dirty water, or a gas, such as carbon dioxide.

▼ *As vehicles burn fuel, such as gasoline, they also produce waste gases that pollute the air.*

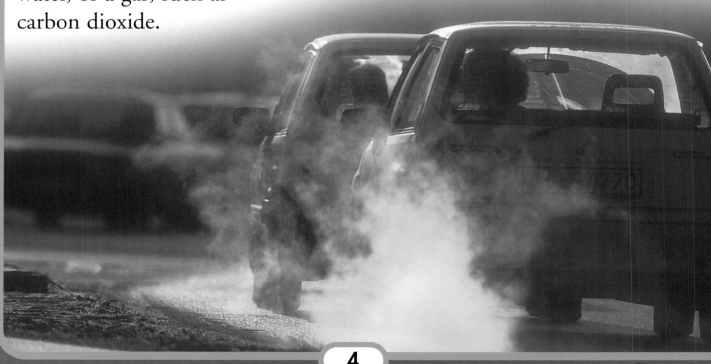

The good news is that most waste contains valuable materials that can be used again. This is called recycling. Recycling takes a little effort, but it really helps to solve the problem of waste disposal. Everyone can help by recycling and reducing waste.

▲ Taking used bottles, tin cans, and paper to recycling centers so they can be used again helps to reduce the problem of waste disposal.

LOOK CLOSER

Litter is any garbage that is just dumped instead of being disposed of safely. It spoils the look of places and can harm wildlife. Litter causes problems even on tropical islands like the one shown here.

Household waste

Every one of us has produced all kinds of waste since we got up this morning. It's not just the wrappers we put in the garbage can–we also produce waste each time we turn on the computer or brush our teeth.

In rich countries, each home produces at least a garbage can of trash each week. A lot of this is food packaging, such as tin cans and bottles. We also throw away leftover food, newspapers, clothes, and grass clippings. Machines we use in the home, like computers, run on electricity. Often, this has been made in power plants that create harmful waste.

▼ In rich countries, the garbage we produce is collected every week, so we don't have to think about it. But it all has to be disposed of.

other 7%
food 7%
wood 7%
glass 7%
metal 8%
plastic 8%
plants 18%
paper 38%

▲ *The garbage we throw away each week is made up of roughly these percentages of waste. Most of it can be recycled.*

As well as the trash in the garbage can, we produce wastewater whenever we wash ourselves, our clothes, or dishes, or go to the bathroom. In rich countries, some of this dirty water is cleaned in sewage plants, so it is safe to use again. In poorer countries, the polluted water often empties into lakes and rivers, where it can do harm to wildlife.

CLOSE TO HOME

Batteries used to power radios, flashlights, and personal stereos are made from chemicals. These produce poisonous waste that lasts for many centuries. If dumped carelessly, batteries harm nature, but they can now be recycled.

Problem packaging

Much of the garbage we throw away each week is food packaging, mainly cardboard cartons but also tin cans and bottles. In the last 20 years or so, the food we buy from supermarkets has come with more and more packaging. This adds to the problem of waste disposal.

◄ It is lots of fun getting new toys. Often, though, these products come in too much packaging and have been made in faraway countries.

In poorer countries, people buy fresh foods grown locally from the nearest market. In rich countries, supermarkets sell foods from all over the world. These goods are packaged to keep them safe on the long trip to the supermarket and to make them look more attractive.

CLOSE TO HOME

Next time your family goes shopping, take a look at all the packaging. For example, clothes often have just one layer of packaging, breakfast cereals have several layers, and fancy goods, like a box of chocolates, have the most of all.

▼ *Bright packaging on supermarket shelves is designed to tempt us into buying the products.*

Packaging is often made from valuable materials: cardboard is made from trees, glass from minerals, and plastic from oil. Energy is used to make packaging, and the process may cause pollution. In addition, transporting goods uses fuel, which creates pollution.

Waste disposal

Have you ever wondered what happens to the waste that is collected from your garbage can? It usually ends up in large pits called landfills, like 90 percent of the world's waste.

At landfills, garbage is packed down, then regularly covered with layers of soil. When the pit is full, a thicker layer of soil is added. Then the site may be reused as a park or golf course. The problem is that many countries are running out of land that can be used for landfills.

◀ A truck dumps its load of garbage into a landfill. Sometimes poisonous chemicals leak out from these sites to pollute nearby land.

Rotting garbage gives off a gas called methane. Pipes are sunk into landfills to release this gas. It can then be used as fuel. Garbage itself can also provide fuel. It is sometimes burned in huge ovens called incinerators, and the heat is used to generate electricity. However, the incinerators produce a lot of ash that still has to be buried in landfills.

▲ The oven in an incinerator must be very hot to burn plastic. If it is too cool, poisonous gases called dioxins are released.

LOOK CLOSER

At small biogas plants like this one in Africa, grass, dung, and water are mixed to produce manure and methane. The manure is used to fertilize fields. The methane provides energy for cooking.

Rotten garbage

Some types of garbage biodegrade, or rot, quickly. Other waste—mainly man-made materials—takes hundreds of years to decay or doesn't rot at all.

Things made from natural materials, such as paper, wood, wool, and cotton, rot quickly. They are said to be biodegradable. When plants and animals die, their remains are eaten and broken down by worms, beetles, fungi, and tiny bacteria. This process returns the goodness that the dead plants and animals contain to the soil, where it nourishes more plants.

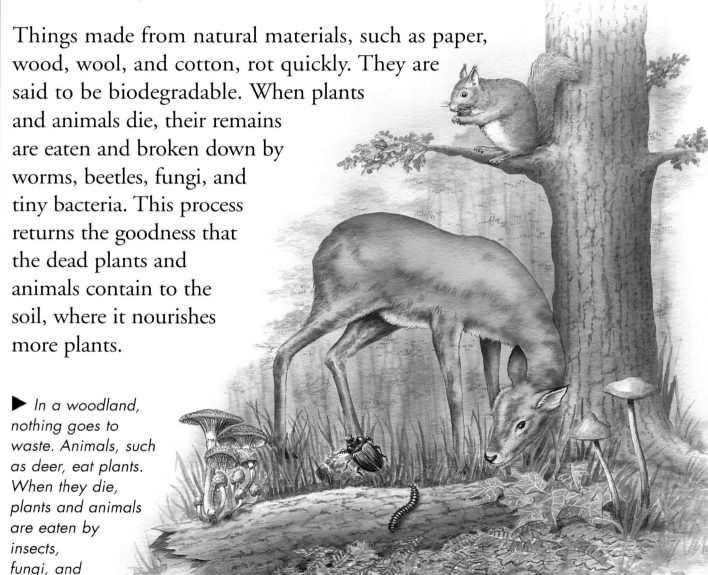

▶ In a woodland, nothing goes to waste. Animals, such as deer, eat plants. When they die, plants and animals are eaten by insects, fungi, and bacteria.

Artificial materials, such as plastic, metal, and glass, aren't biodegradable—they don't decay or decay very slowly. This makes them useful as building or storage materials, but it becomes a problem when we want to throw them away. Most of these materials, however, can be reused or recycled, so they shouldn't just be thrown away.

The litter you see on beaches provides a clue to the materials that rot and don't rot quickly. Next time you visit a beach, look to see what kinds of litter are washed up.

◀ *Plastic litter spoils the landscape until someone clears it up.*

Farm waste

Farms produce a lot of waste that rots quickly. On traditional farms, it is recycled. However, many modern farms now produce waste that does not decay and is highly poisonous.

Farms produce natural waste, such as leftover plant stems and animal dung. This waste decays quickly to form manure, which is useful. Traditionally, farmers spread manure on their fields as fertilizer. Farms that use this method reduce their waste.

▼ A tractor sprays manure on fields to fertilize them. In this way, waste is used again.

▶ A helicopter sprays chemical pesticides onto fields to kill pests, such as insects.

In rich countries, many farms now use chemicals instead of manure as fertilizer. This method produces bumper crops but causes a waste-disposal problem. The leftover chemicals pollute the soil and water supplies and harm animals.

LOOK CLOSER

Tiny plants called algae thrive in water polluted by fertilizer or wastewater from houses. As the algae grow, they make the water green and cloudy. When sunlight cannot filter through the water, animals, such as fish, suffer. The algae also use up all the water's oxygen, which harms water life.

Industrial waste

Mines, factories, and power plants produce far more waste than all the buildings in crowded cities. Solid, liquid, and gas waste from industry may pollute the air, water, or land.

The mining of metals and fuel is vital for industry and manufacturing. However, when metals are mined, vast amounts of waste rock and dust are left behind. This waste, called tailings, contains metals and other substances that pollute the landscape. The factories that process the raw materials also produce a lot of waste.

▼ This bauxite mine in Venezuela has been built on rain forest land. Waste from the mine harms forest life.

Power plants burn fuels to make electricity. In the process, they release waste gases, such as carbon dioxide, into the air. These gases act as a blanket that traps the Sun's heat near Earth's surface. This is causing Earth's climate to get warmer, an effect known as global warming.

◀ *Liquid waste from a factory in Mexico pollutes the local canal.*

CLOSE TO HOME

Tin cans that contain carbonated drinks are usually made of steel or a light, strong metal called aluminum. Aluminum is made from a mineral called bauxite. Tropical forests and other wild areas are being cleared to make way for new bauxite mines. When this happens, local wildlife is destroyed.

Dangerous waste

Some factories and power plants produce toxic, or poisonous, waste that is very difficult to get rid of. These poisons remain dangerous for hundreds, even thousands, of years.

Nuclear waste is one of the most dangerous types of waste. The rays it gives off can kill people and wildlife. Nuclear waste is produced by power plants, which use a metal called uranium to make energy. Less dangerous waste from these power plants is released into the air or buried at sea. The most deadly waste is stored underground in sealed drums.

◀ A worker shifts a drum containing nuclear waste at a special burial site in the United States.

◀ When toxic waste is dumped at sea, it often leaks and builds up in the bodies of large creatures, such as beluga whales, killing them.

Factories that make paint, soap, cosmetics, plastic, fertilizers, and medicines also produce toxic waste. If this is buried underground, it sometimes seeps into local water supplies and makes people sick. Some towns built on these sites have been torn down after people living in them became ill.

LOOK CLOSER

Old-style refrigerators contain dangerous chemicals called chlorofluorocarbons (CFCs), which harm the layer of ozone gas high in the air that screens us from harmful rays in sunlight. CFCs were banned in 1987, and new refrigerators don't contain them. This ban has had some effect on restoring ozone. CFCs have to be taken out of old refrigerators. Often there are stockpiles of old refrigerators waiting for this to happen.

Rich or poor

Some countries produce more waste than others. People from wealthy regions, like North America and Europe, generally create far more waste than people from poorer places, such as India and Africa.

Rich countries produce a lot of waste, in part because people living there have more money to spend on new products. When machinery breaks down, it is often easier to throw it away than to get it repaired. We also use energy wastefully. Rich countries are now concerned about pollution and waste disposal, and some governments have introduced strict laws to control pollution.

◄ *Heavily packaged foods like hamburgers, fries, and soft drinks are very popular in rich countries.*

In poorer parts of the world, people have less money to spend on new goods, so they reuse and repair things. Recycling is a way of life. Cardboard, plastic, and bottles are all carefully cleaned, sorted, and used again. However, pollution controls are often less strict, so some towns, farms, and factories release dangerous waste into the environment.

▲ *In poor countries, some people earn a living by rummaging through garbage at landfills in search of things to sell or reuse.*

LOOK CLOSER

In various parts of the world, people use and throw away very different amounts of paper. The average person in the United States uses over 660 lb of paper in a year. In the UK, people use about 365 lb. In India, people use just 6.5 lb of paper in a year.

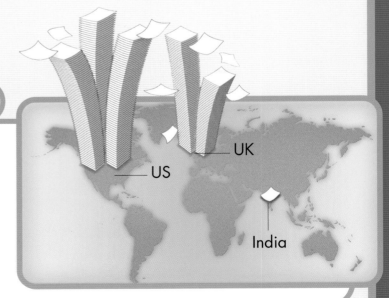

UK

US

India

Recycling waste

All the waste we throw away is steadily building up to clutter and harm our planet. What can be done about it? Recycling is part of the answer to the growing problem of waste.

Recycling not only cuts down on waste, but it can also save energy and useful resources. Glass is easy to recycle. It is made by melting sand and limestone in a furnace. Recycled glass is smashed up and then reheated. This process uses less energy than making new glass and helps to save sand and limestone.

▲ *A truck dumps a load of broken glass, called cullet, for recycling. Beforehand, the glass is sorted into different colors, which are melted down separately.*

Paper and cardboard are also easy to recycle. These are made from wood. Trees that provide wood for paper are grown in special plantations, often on land that was once wasteland or marshland. Recycling paper helps to save trees and wild land. It also saves energy, which is used when trees are felled and wood is made into paper.

▼ *A forester prepares lumber for transport to the sawmill, where it will be pulped for paper.*

CLOSE TO HOME

Paper and cardboard can be reused at home, as well as recycled. Envelopes can be reused by putting a gummed label over the address. Old Christmas and birthday cards can be made into gift tags. Always write on both sides of a sheet of paper before recycling it.

Reuse or recycle

C loth, metal, and plastic can all be recycled to ease the problem of waste disposal. Always think if something can be repaired or reused before throwing it away!

Metals, such as iron, steel, and aluminum, can be recycled any number of times. The used metal is simply reheated and remolded to make new objects, from steel girders to paper clips. The process cuts down on waste and pollution from mining and saves energy. For example, making tin cans from recycled steel uses only a quarter of the energy used to make cans from fresh steel.

◀ At recycling plants, plastic is shredded into tiny pieces before being melted down and used again.

◀ In poor countries, where metal is prized, people are skilled at finding new uses for metal objects. This man is sitting on a steel chair made from old tire rims.

CLOSE TO HOME

Many products have symbols printed on them to show that they can be recycled. Next time you go shopping, look for recycling symbols, such as the ones shown below. They all mean that the packaging can be recycled.

Old cloth can also be recycled. It is ripped apart and cleaned. The recycled fibers can then be woven into new cloth or used to stuff mattresses. Plastic is harder to recycle, since there are many different kinds that cannot be mixed. However, an amazing number of objects can now be made from recycled plastic. For example, fleece jackets can be made from plastic bottles.

How can we help?

We can all help to tackle the problem of waste by following the three "Rs": Reduce, Reuse, and Recycle. Reduce waste by buying goods with less packaging. Reuse items, such as glass jars and plastic bags. Recycle the rest!

Today, many countries have set up recycling programs to save resources and reduce the amount of waste they have to deal with. Governments have also made laws to cut waste pollution from farms and factories. Campaign groups, such as Greenpeace, have helped to stop the dumping of poisonous waste.

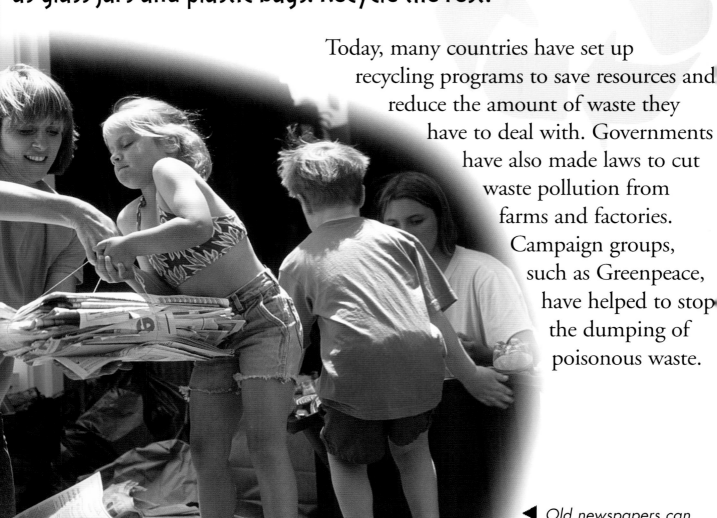

◄ *Old newspapers can be collected and taken to a recycling center. Never throw them away!*

Take advantage of local programs by recycling used paper, cardboard, metal, plastic, glass, and cloth. Clean these materials and bag them. Take old toys, books, and clothes to charity shops, where they can be resold to raise money. When you go shopping, look for labels that show that items, such as toilet paper rolls, have been made from recycled materials. Reuse things like plastic bags and glass jars, too.

▲ *Recycling takes a bit more time, but if we all do it, it really will help to reduce waste.*

In the yard, start a compost heap using old wooden boxes or a garbage can with holes drilled in the bottom. Put in natural waste, like vegetable peelings, which will rot on the heap to make a rich compost. This can then be used to fertilize flowers.

◀ *The waste on a compost heap decays, forming a natural fertilizer.*

Waste projects

Investigate the types of garbage that decay quickly and those that don't by conducting the simple experiment shown here. You can also use old newspapers, cardboard, plastic cups, corks, and balloons to make beautiful masks.

▲ *Natural materials, such as apples, decay quickly. They are broken down by insects and bacteria.*

WILL IT ROT?

Find out more about the kinds of garbage that do and don't rot by burying garbage in pots. You could use old yogurt containers or flowerpots.

1. Put different kinds of garbage in each pot. Include natural materials, such as fruit, vegetable peelings, wood, or paper. Put man-made materials, such as a small plastic toy or a potato chip bag, glass marbles, and metal screws in other pots.

2. Use a trowel to cover each item of garbage with damp soil, then store the pots in a damp place outside. Label each pot to show what it contains.

3. After a month, remove the soil to find out which items have decayed. Has anything disappeared altogether? What has happened to the metal? Are there any changes to the glass or plastic? Write down your results in a notebook.

MAKING MASKS FROM JUNK

Use trash, including old newspapers and plastic cups, to make masks for yourself and your friends, perhaps for a party. You will also need paste made from flour and water, scissors, a balloon, rubber bands, poster paints, and corks.

1. The basic masks are made from papier-mâché. Blow up a balloon and tear newspaper into strips. Soak the strips in paste and cover the balloon with at least four layers of strips.

2. Leave the papier-mâché for a day or two, until completely dry. Now pop the balloon. Cut the papier-mâché ball in half to make two masks. Measure and cut holes for your eyes and mouth.

▼ Attach rubber bands to the back so you can wear your fantastic mask.

3. Plan your mask: it could be an animal, a clown, or a pirate. Cover the papier-mâché with several layers of paint. Glue on construction paper or plastic strips for ears, teeth, and a tongue and stick on a plastic cup or cork for the nose.

Ask an adult to help you when using scissors.

CAMPAIGN GROUPS

Friends of the Earth
1025 Vermont Ave., NW, Suite 300, Washington, D.C. 20005

Greenpeace
702 H Street, NW, Suite 300
Washington, D.C. 20001

World Wildlife Fund
1250 24th Street, NW
Washington, D.C.
20037-1175

WASTE AND RECYCLING WEBSITES

US Environment Protection Agency: www.epa.gov/students
Environment Explorers' Club: www.epa.gov/kids
Wastewatch UK: www.wastewatch.org.uk

OTHER INFORMATION WEBSITES

www.georesources.co.uk
www.thomasrecycling.com/kids.html
Kids Recycling: www.kidsrecycle.org
Waste quiz: www.pca.state.mn.us/kids/kidsQuizGarbage.cfm

Waste factfile

• In the 1970s, a former landfill site called Love Canal near Niagara Falls in the United States hit the news. In the 1950s, a housing development and school were built on the site. Then people there began to get sick. The site was found to be poisoned by waste, and the houses had to be torn down.

• The worst disaster involving nuclear waste happened at a site called Kyshtym in Russia in 1957. An explosion at a nuclear storage site scattered radioactive waste over a vast region covering 5,800 sq. miles. Full details of the accident are not known, but many people probably died.

• In 1975, the American company 3M launched a campaign called "Pollution Prevention Pays" to reduce waste. It put into practice 1,200 ideas for cutting waste and pollution. Ten years later, the company had halved its waste production and saved nearly 500 million dollars.

• The United States produces more waste than any other country. With only 5 percent of the world's population, it produces 19 percent of the world's waste. However, the United States is better at recycling than many other countries. The United States recycles 25 percent of its domestic waste, whereas the UK, for example, only manages to recycle 12 percent.

• Steel is the world's most recycled metal. The steel produced today is made from about 40 percent recycled metal.

Glossary

Biodegradable
A biodegradable substance rots, for example, plant and animal waste.

Bacteria
Microscopic single-celled life forms.

Biogas
A gas given off by plant and animal waste as they rot.

Cullet
Smashed glass that can be remelted to make new glass.

Fuel
A substance that can be burned to release energy in the form of light and heat.

Global warming
Warming weather worldwide, caused by the increase of gases in the air, such as carbon dioxide, that trap the Sun's heat.

Incinerator
A very hot furnace in which garbage is burned, often to generate electricity.

Landfill
A pit in the ground where garbage is dumped and then covered with soil.

Methane
A gas given off by rotting garbage, which can be burned to provide energy.

Mineral
A nonliving chemical substance.

Nonbiodegradable
A nonbiodegradable substance does not rot, for example, plastic and glass.

Pesticides
Chemicals that farmers spray on fields to kill crop-harming pests, such as insects.

Pollution
Harmful waste substances.

Radioactive
A radioactive material gives off dangerous radiation.

Recycling
The process of reclaiming useful materials from waste. The materials are either used again or made into new products.

Resources
Materials, such as wood, oil, and metal, that are used to make things.

Sewage plant
Place where used, dirty water is filtered and cleaned so it is safe and can be used again.

Index